SKIING
is for me

Annette Jo Chappell

photographs by
Alan Oddie

 Lerner Publications Company   Minneapolis

The author would like to thank the students and staff at Chilao Mountain School in LaCanada, California; the management team at Mount Waterman; and Colleen Schwitzgebel and Joyce Parkel.

Photographs on pages 44 and 45 © Focus on Sports. Used by permission.

Lowell A. Dickmeyer, Series Editor

LIBRARY OF CONGRESS CATALOGING IN PUBLICATION DATA

Chappell, Annette Jo.
Skiing is for me.

(A Sports for Me Book)
SUMMARY: A young boy describes how he learned the techniques of downhill skiing.

1. Skis and skiing—Juvenile literature. [1. Skis and skiing]
I. Oddie, Alan. II. Title.

GV854.C513 1978   796.9′3   78-12411
ISBN 0-8225-1082-0

Manufactured in the United States of America.
Published simultaneously in Canada by J. M. Dent & Sons (Canada) Ltd., Don Mills, Ontario.

International Standard Book Number: 0-8225-1082-0
Library of Congress Catalog Card Number: 78-12411

2   3   4   5   6   7   8   9   10   85   84   83   82   81   80

Hello, I'm Steven. I just got back from my first skiing trip in the mountains. I can't wait to go again! I had so much fun learning how to ski. Downhill skiing is just about the most exciting sport I know.

Downhill skiing is the kind of skiing where you zigzag down a hill or mountain. I got a thrill just from being in the white snow and feeling the fresh air on my face. You can see from these pictures why skiing is called an action sport.

I'd like to tell you about my first skiing adventure. The idea for my ski trip came up a few weeks ago. Some of Dad's friends invited me to spend a week with them at Mount Waterman. They had a son, Eric, who was my age.

Dad thought that a visit would be a great chance for me to learn how to ski. We made plans to go over my winter break so I wouldn't miss any school. But I planned to go to ski school while I was at Mount Waterman.

I had only two weeks to get ready for my trip. In that time, I wanted to learn as much as I could about skiing. So I went to the public library and borrowed some books on the sport. I was surprised to see so many skiing books on the shelves.

As I was looking through the books, Dad came in. He smiled and said, "Reading about how to ski is good, but you should be getting your body in shape, too. If you are in good physical condition, you won't be as likely to have sore or strained muscles after long hours on the slopes." He showed me some exercises that would get me in shape.

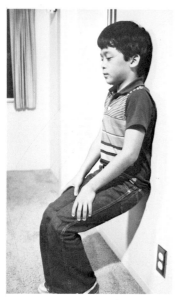

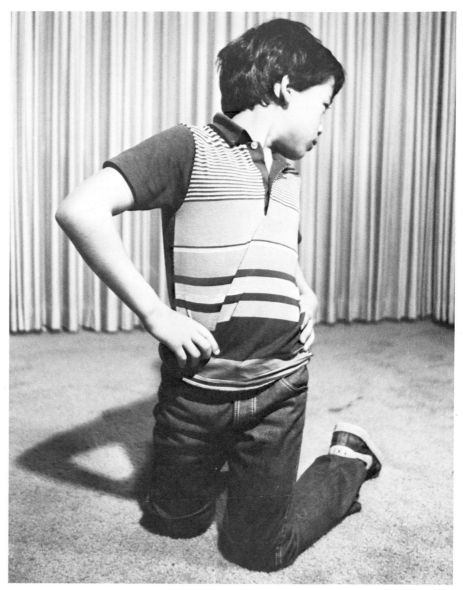

I exercised every day. I did leg lifts and twists, and I leaned against a wall. I did some running, too. These exercises made my leg and stomach muscles stronger. Exercise also helped my balance and body control.

Dad showed me how to use his old bongo board. This is a wooden plank set across a round wooden log. Standing on the bongo board gave me practice balancing, and it strengthened my legs. It took me a while to learn how to use the board without slipping off. But it was fun.

I also spent some time planning which clothes to take on my ski trip. Dad said that the main thing is to have clothes that are warm, but not bulky. You have to be able to move around easily.

It is important to wear clothes that resist water so you can stay dry. Mom took me shopping for special ski pants, which are waterproof. They are also warmer than regular jeans. You can wear jeans skiing, but you should remember to brush the snow off them right away to keep from getting wet. I already had a parka that was water-proof. The gloves I was taking along were also waterproof. You should not wear knit mittens if you can help it. They get wet easily and aren't warm enough. Skiing is no fun if you are cold.

My suitcase was packed for two days before I had to leave. Finally the day came when we drove to Mount Waterman. As we went higher up into the mountains, I could see the snowy peaks getting closer and closer. What a view! I had never seen so much snow!

It was late in the day when I finally met Eric and his family. Within a short time, Eric and I were talking like old friends. He told me about life in the mountains.

I could hardly sleep that night as I looked forward to my first day on skis. It was still early when Eric woke me.

After breakfast, Eric and his father took me to the ski shop at the lodge. That was where I would rent my ski gear. I needed skis, boots, poles and bindings. Eric had extra equipment, but his gear did not fit me well enough. It is important that ski equipment fits exactly. Not only will it be more comfortable, but it will be safer, too.

First I was fitted for skis. Properly fitted skis should be no taller than your head. The curved part of the ski is called the **tip**, and the other end is the **tail**. The sides of the ski are called **edges**. Skis are flexible because they are made of special hard plastic called **fiberglass**.

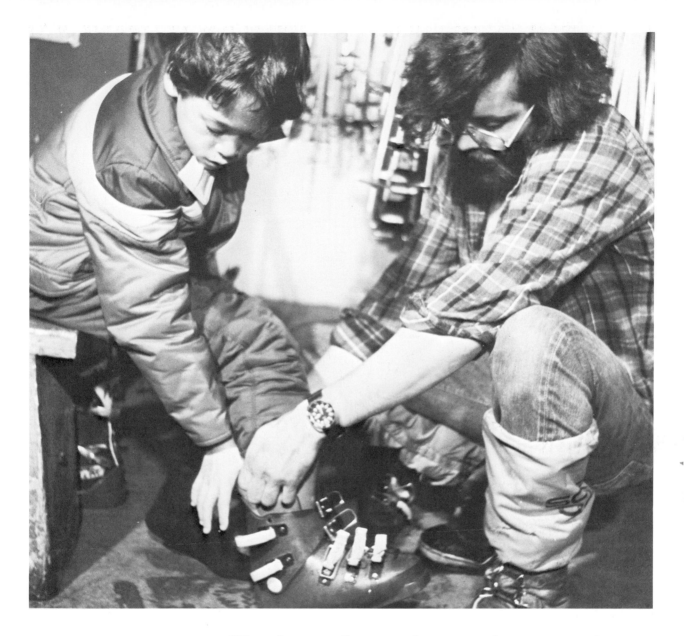

The boots I rented were the same size as my regular shoes. Your toes should have enough room to wiggle. Your heels should be snug against the backs of the boots. At the top of the boot, you should have enough room to put a finger between your ankle and the boot.

Ski boots are tilted at the ankles so that you have to lean forward. The boots help to keep your weight forward. This is important when you ski. I also found out that ski boots are really heavy.

Bindings hold the boots to the skis. There are many different kinds of bindings. I liked the ones that snapped on easily as I stepped onto my skis.

Bindings are very important because they protect you from injury when you fall. If you should fall, the bindings will release your skis. This release action prevents broken ankles and legs.

The shop attendant also clipped safety straps to my ankles. When you fall and your bindings release, the safety straps keep your skis from sliding away from you. Loose skis could be dangerous to other skiers on the slope below you.

Next I picked out my poles. They are used for balance and to help you move forward. Your poles should pass easily under your arm pits. The bottom of the pole is called the **point**. Above the point is a **basket**, which keeps the pole from going too far into the snow. The long metal part of the pole is called the **shaft**. At the top is the **handle**. Your hands go through the handle straps to prevent your poles from getting away during a fall.

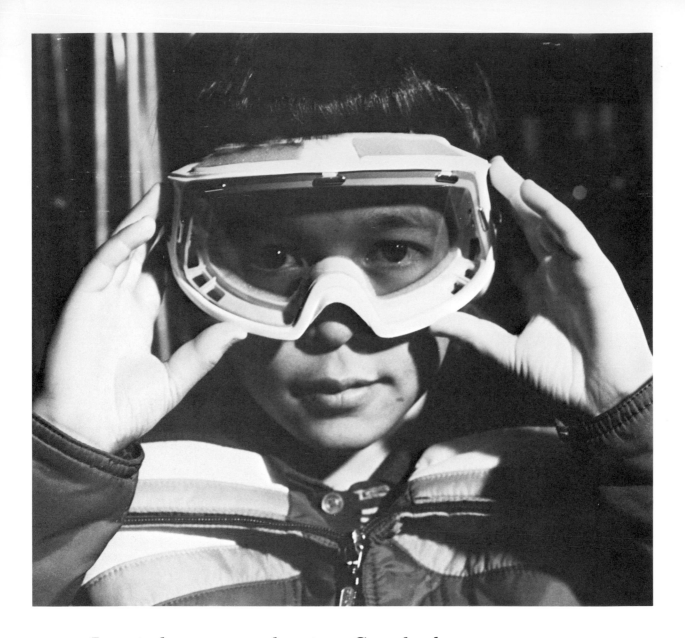

I rented some goggles, too. Goggles keep
the wind and snow out of the eyes. They also
help to cut down glare from the sun.

It took a long time to get properly fitted
for all of my ski equipment. Eric agreed
that it might seem like a lot of trouble, but
safe gear is the first step toward safe skiing.

After getting all of my equipment, I went to my first ski lesson.

My skiing instructor was named Cheryl. She seemed happy and friendly. I also met the other students in the class. Most of them had never skied before.

First we learned how to stand on our skis. Cheryl said, "Keep your feet slightly apart, weight forward and equal on both feet, ankles bent forward, and head up." We all got into position and looked at Cheryl.

Our next step was to walk on our skis. Cheryl showed us how to glide forward in short steps with our knees bent. The skis should not be lifted from the snow. The push off is done with both arms and poles working against the snow. This is called **poling**. It almost feels like skating.

Then we learned how to turn around on flat ground. One way is the **kick turn**. Using your poles for balance, you lift one ski high and place it back down in the opposite direction. Then you lift the other ski and swing it around until the two skis are together.

An easier way to turn is the **star turn**. Instead of turning all at once, you take several steps to change directions. First you lift the tip of one ski and move it over, forming a V with your skis. Then you bring the other ski next to the first one. These two steps are repeated until you have turned as far as you want.

Shane went first when we learned to walk uphill. He turned his side to the hill and then moved up, one ski at a time. The uphill ski was moved first. Then he followed with the other ski. This way of moving uphill is called **side-stepping**. Cheryl reminded Shane to lean uphill to help keep his balance.

The **herringbone** is another way of moving uphill. It is called a herringbone because it leaves funny tracks in the snow that look like the spine bones of a fish. When doing the herringbone, you point the tips of your skis away from each other and move up the hill one step at a time. As you climb, be sure to dig the inside edges of your skis into the snow.

We spent a long time learning how to fall. Cheryl said that learning to fall safely was just as important as learning to ski. She said that falling wouldn't hurt if it was done right. The important thing to remember is to relax. Fighting a fall will only make it worse.

When you fall on the slopes, try to land to the side of your skis and not on top of them. Get your poles out of the way, too. When a fall is very rough, your skis will be released automatically. After you have stopped, the skis can be quickly clamped on again. It takes no time at all to start skiing again after a fall.

Cheryl told us a neat trick to use in getting up after a fall. Keep your skis sideways to the hill. Then, bend your knees and bring your body close to your skis. Finally, put both poles above the uphill ski and push yourself up to a standing position.

After practicing the basics for a while, we were finally ready to go up the mountain. We had to use a **chairlift** to get to the top of the slope. But first we watched some experienced skiers use the chairlift. As we watched, Cheryl gave us some tips for getting on and off.

"When you are ready to ride, stand with your back to the chair. As the chair approaches you, grab the center bar and sit down. Remember to keep the tips of your skis up. Otherwise they could catch in the snow and cause you to fall forward. When it is time to get off, simply stand up and push off. You will glide forward. Remember to keep moving to get out of the way of the skiers on the chairs behind you."

When Cheryl had finished, we each found a partner for the ride. Cheryl was my partner. I followed her instructions and was soon in the air. The ride was beautiful! I could see skiers on the slopes below me.

When we reached the top, we followed Cheryl to the **bunny hill**. Bunny hills are small slopes for beginning skiers. Intermediate hills are a little steeper. Advanced slopes are very steep and fast.

Cheryl told us never to try a slope that is too steep for our abilities. This made sense to me. She also told us about some other rules for safe conduct on the slopes. The downhill skier has the right of way. You should look out for skiers on the hill below you. Stay well out of their way. Do not ski so fast that you lose control.

We kept these rules in mind while Cheryl taught us the **snowplow**. The snowplow is a good beginning skiing technique. To do the snowplow, you bend your knees and shift your weight forward so that it is equal on both feet. Put the tips of your skis close together. The tails of your skis should be far apart, forming a **V**. Keep your poles back.

To stop, shift your weight to the inside edges of your skis. Press out with your heels to widen the space between your tails. Bring your poles forward to help you stop.

Turning was really easy. To turn right, we shifted our weight to our left feet. To turn left, we put more weight on our right feet.

Ski school was over for the day, but I kept on practicing the snowplow until the lifts closed. There were other skiers on the beginners' slopes who were also practicing skiing, stopping, and turning. Everyone was having fun.

I was very tired after my first day on the slopes. I was sore, too. My leg muscles hurt the most. Eric told me that it is normal to feel very tired after a full day of skiing. He said that I would get used to it. I had no trouble falling asleep that night.

The next three days went pretty much like the first. Every day I practiced what I had learned until the lifts closed. Moves that seemed hard at first became easier with practice. I fell down many times, but I didn't get hurt because I wasn't going very fast.

There were so many nice people on the mountain. They were always friendly and ready to help when I had problems.

Every day I learned new skills. I learned a new method of turning called the **stem christie**. When you do a stem christie, one ski is angled as in the snowplow, and the other ski is straight. You turn in the direction that the angled ski is pointed.

Soon I progressed to **parallel** skiing. Most skiers use this method. When you parallel ski, both skis are kept close together and pointed forward. Cheryl thought I did well to learn this so quickly.

Parallel turns are made with the skis together. When you want to turn, reach forward and plant the inside pole near the top of the skis. Take your weight off your heels and push on your downhill ski as your hip swings in the direction you want to turn.

You do not have to ski straight down a slope when you parallel ski. You can ski back and forth across the slope instead. This is called **traversing**.

The days passed quickly for me. Friday was a holiday, so ski school was closed. Since this was going to be my last day in the mountains, I looked forward to skiing all day with Eric.

Eric and I rested when we got tired. Sometimes we stopped at the snack bar for a drink. I was always thirsty after all that exercise.

Once as Eric and I walked back to the slopes, we saw the Ski Patrol. The Ski Patrol is a group of expert skiers who give help and first aid to skiers who have had accidents. But when Eric and I saw the Patrol, there hadn't been an accident. The Patrol was just giving a few of my classmates some advice.

After skiing some more, Eric took me to the east side of the mountain. An adult ski competition was taking place. It was really exciting to watch.

The first race we saw was called a **slalom**. In the slalom race, the skiers zigzagged down the mountain in and out of a long row

of flags. The skiers raced against the clock, and the one with the fastest time won.

There was also a downhill race. The skiers in this race followed a course down the mountain. They tried to cross the finish line in the shortest time possible.

The event I liked best was the ski jumping competition. Skiers took turns jumping off a long ramp that curved up slightly at the end. It was thrilling to see them sailing through the air. The one who jumped the greatest distance won the event.

Eric and I had a little more time to ski before the lifts closed for the day. As I took my last run down the mountain, the wind blew against my face and the snow swished under my skis. I felt free and happy. I knew it would not be long before I would return to the mountains for more skiing.

Words about SKIING

BINDINGS: The part of your gear that holds the boots to the skis. The bindings release the boots during a fall.

BUNNY HILL: A small slope where beginners ski

DOWNHILL RACING: A form of high speed competition in which the racers ski one at a time down a marked course in the shortest possible time

EDGE: To set the edges of the skis into the snow at an angle to the slope

GOGGLES: Heavy plastic eye coverings that keep out wind, snow, and glare

HERRINGBONE: A method of walking uphill on skis that are in a **V** formation. The tips of the skis are pointed away from each other as the skier steps up the hill.

MOGULS: The bumps of snow on a slope

PARALLEL SKIING: A method of skiing keeping both skis close together

POLING: A method of walking on skis by pushing yourself forward with your poles

POWDER: Light, dry snow

ROPE TOW: A heavy rope that pulls skiers up to the top of a slope

SIDE-STEPPING: A method of walking uphill one step at a time with your side to the slope

SLALOM: A type of ski race in which skiers speed downhill, turning in and out of poles placed at intervals down the course

SNOWPLOW: A method of skiing in which the front tips of the skis are angled toward each other, forming a V-shaped wedge

STAR TURN: A method of turning on flat ground by a series of mini-turns. First the skier lifts the tip of one ski and moves it over a short distance. Then the other ski is lifted around until the two skis are together. These two steps are repeated until the skier has turned far enough.

STEM CHRISTIE: A method of turning in which one ski is held at an angle and the other ski is kept straight

TAIL: The back of a ski

TIP: The turned-up end of a ski

TRAVERSE: To ski across the face of a hill rather than straight down it

ABOUT THE AUTHOR

ANNETTE JO CHAPPELL is a ski instructor at Mount Waterman in Southern California, where this book was photographed. She also serves as tennis director at the Field House Racquet Club in Thousand Oaks, California, and is the sports director at Newbury Park, a major sporting complex in the area.

ABOUT THE PHOTOGRAPHER

ALAN ODDIE was born and raised in Scotland. He now resides in Santa Monica, California. In addition to his work as a photographer, Mr. Oddie is an author and a producer of educational filmstrips. He is currently the staff photographer for *Franciscan Communications*.